I Know There Are So Many of You

T0056385

# I Know There Are So Many of You

## Alain Badiou

Translated by Susan Spitzer

polity

First published in French as *Je vous sais si nombreux . . .* © Librairie Arthème Fayard, 2017

This English edition © Polity Press, 2019

Polity Press
65 Bridge Street
Cambridge CB2 1UR, UK

Polity Press
101 Station Landing
Suite 300
Medford, MA 02155, USA

ISBN-13: 978-1-5095-3259-9 (hardback)
ISBN-13: 978-1-5095-3260-5 (paperback)

A catalogue record for this book is available from the British Library.

Library of Congress Cataloging-in-Publication Data

Names: Badiou, Alain, author.
Title: I know there are so many of you / Alain Badiou.
Other titles: Je vous sais si nombreux. English.
Description: Cambridge, UK ; Medford, MA : Polity Press, 2018. | Includes bibliographical references and index.
Identifiers: LCCN 2018004916 (print) | LCCN 2018020846 (ebook) | ISBN 9781509532629 (Epub) | ISBN 9781509532599 (hardback) | ISBN 9781509532605 (pbk.)
Subjects: LCSH: Humanity--Philosophy. | Humanism. | Other (Philosophy) | Young adults--Political activity. | Political science--Philosophy.
Classification: LCC BJ1533.H9 (ebook) | LCC BJ1533.H9 B3413 2018 (print) | DDC 194--dc23
LC record available at https://lccn.loc.gov/2018004916

Typeset in 12.5 on 15 pt Adobe Garamond by
Servis Filmsetting Ltd, Stockport, Cheshire
Printed and bound in Great Britain by Clays Ltd, Elcograf S.p.A.

For further information on Polity, visit our website: politybooks.com

# Contents

# Preface

The two essays that make up this volume began as two lectures I delivered, the first at the Lycée Henri-IV and the second at the École nationale des Beaux-Arts. A common feature of both was that they were addressed to audiences composed predominantly of young people, although for different reasons. At the high school the reason was obvious, since there are not many old people still in high school. At Beaux-Arts it was a different story, because it didn't involve students from that school, at least not primarily, but rather a very informal "organization" of young and not-so-young people, almost all of whom were from the recent, closely related mass movements, the Nuit Debout ["Night on Our Feet"] gathering on the

Place de la République and the fight against the labor law devised by the final Valls-Hollande government. They met regularly at Beaux-Arts to assess their action and to plan for the future. The organization was called "Conséquences," which is a good name.

I owed my presence as a speaker to the mediation and requests of two young friends of mine, each of whom was from one of the places concerned and who basically represented for me the appeal to young people of philosophy primarily, in the one case, and of politics primarily, in the other.

In both cases there was a full house, an audience listening intently, and intense discussion afterward.

The key concept of the first lecture was the Other and of the second one, politics. You'll see fairly quickly, I believe, that there were subtle, close links between the two requests. Basically, the situation very naturally turned the two lectures into a kind of sequel to my recently published book *La vraie vie* [published in English as *The True Life,* Polity, 2017], which was itself based for the most part on lectures to high-school students.

So once again it was a case, as the Athenian

citizens' characterization of Socrates' public speeches had it, of "corrupting the youth," which means: offering them some possibility, if not of changing the world, at least of having a strong enough desire to see what that could be like.

Alain Badiou

# The Other

Thank you for this large turnout. It's a pleasure for me to be here in this famous establishment and to speak to so many of those I once resembled, even though I was at Louis-le-Grand. I'm only mentioning the old rivalry between Lycée Henri-IV and Lycée Louis-le-Grand because I've managed to get over it, since, as you can see, I'm speaking here at Henri-IV.

I'd like to begin with some banalities. But essential banalities, of the kind that must never be forgotten. There are some things that are perfectly ordinary and banal, but, for just this reason, they are forgotten, and the forgetting causes damage to sophisticated or fundamental thought. So, since we are going to be talking about the Other,

I'd like to start with some banalities about the Same. Indeed, I'm going to start with a very basic materialist definition of what we all are, namely, members of a well-defined animal species, the human species. This is a very recent species, actually, from the perspective of the overall history of life on our little, insignificant planet. At any rate no more than 200,000 years old, at the most, whereas the existence of living beings on Earth is measured in hundreds of millions of years.

What are the most general characteristics of this recent species?

As you know, the biological criterion of a species, including our own, is that the mating of a male and a female of the species can produce fertile offspring. Now, this obviously happens frequently where the human species is concerned, regardless of the color, the geographical origin, the size, the ideas, or the social organization of the partners. That's the first point.

Furthermore – and this is the second point – the human lifespan, another material criterion, seems unable for the time being to exceed 130 years at the most. All this you know. But it already allows us to make two comments, which, while very simple, are, I believe, fundamental.

The first is that the cosmic adventure, so to speak, of the human species, of the human animal, is actually short. This is a hard thing to imagine because, for us, 200,000 years is already something that's lost in thick mists, especially in comparison with the paltry one-hundred-some-odd years by which our individual life adventure is strictly bounded. Nevertheless, we must still remember this platitude: compared to the overall history of life, the period of existence of the species *Homo sapiens* (that's what we rather pretentiously call ourselves) is a very short, unique adventure. It could therefore be argued that we may be only just beginning, that we may be at the very beginning of this unique adventure. This is so as to establish a time scale for the things that can be said and thought about humanity's collective becoming. The dinosaurs, for example, were not very appealing, at least by our standards, but they existed over a truly enormous time scale as compared with our species. That scale is measured not in thousands of years but in hundreds of millions. Humanity as we know it can imagine itself as a sort of scant beginning. But the beginning of what? That will be one of the issues we'll explore.

The second comment is that there is an

undeniable material level, of a biological nature – that of the reproduction of the species, of sexuation, of birth – on which it has been more or less proven that we're all the same. We're all the same, perhaps, on this one level alone. But on this level that exists and is materially fixed. And then there's the issue of death, which occurs within more or less fixed temporal parameters.

So it can be said, without risk of contradiction, that there is a sameness of humanity as such. And in the final analysis, this sameness of humanity must never, and I mean never, be forgotten, regardless of the myriad differences – which we are also going to explore – that naturally exist with respect to countries, genders, cultures, historical commitments, and so on. There is nonetheless a sort of undeniable foundation that constitutes the sameness of humanity as such. And I say this because the question of whether this basic sameness is ultimately represented or representable at the symbolic level, the level of social organization, the level of relations between sameness and otherness, is one that must be considered open, since this basic sameness does in fact exist.

In sum, to think the Other clearly, we must also give the Same its due.

I'll add a third point. There is evidence that humanity's intellectual capacity, too, is most likely an invariable capacity. Of course, there has been *one* fundamental revolution in human history, actually only one, in my opinion, and by far the most important one in the entire history of the human animal: the Neolithic Revolution. In a short period of time, amounting to a few hundred years, humanity invented settled agriculture, the storage of grain in pottery, hence the possibility of a food surplus, hence the existence of a class of people nourished by this surplus and exempted from having to be directly involved in productive work, hence the existence of the state, bolstered by that of metal weapons, and hence, too, writing, which was originally intended for keeping count of cattle producers and collecting taxes. And, in this context, the conservation, transmission, and advancement of technologies of all sorts were very strongly stimulated.

Compared to this change, which occurred a few millennia ago, any other change is actually not very significant for the time being because, in a certain way, we are still within the parameters that were established back then. These included idle ruling classes, an authoritarian state, professional armies, and wars between nations, all of which put us far in advance of the little groups of hunter-gatherers who had previously represented humanity. We are still inside those parameters. We are Neolithic people.

Yet this revolution doesn't mean that we are superior to the human beings from before the Neolithic Revolution in terms of intellectual capacity. We should bear in mind the existence of wall paintings such as those found in the Chauvet Cave, which everyone has heard about, that date from 30,000 years ago, a time when there were most likely still only little groups of hunter-gatherers, well before the Neolithic Revolution. The mere existence of these paintings testifies to the fact that the human animal's reflective, contemplative, idealizing capacity, as well as its technical virtuosity, were already exactly the same as they are today.

So it is not just at the biological and material level that human sameness, through its adventure, must be asserted but no doubt also at the level of what it is intellectually capable of. This basic unity, this biological and mental Same, has always been the chief obstacle to theories holding that humanity is not the same, theories holding that there are fundamentally different subspecies, usually referred to as "races." Racists, as you know, have always feared and banned sexual relations, to say nothing of marriage, between the members of the superior races and those of the inferior races, who nevertheless presented a constant temptation owing to the subterranean work of humanity's unity. They enacted terrible laws to ensure that black men would never have access to white women, or Jewish men to so-called "Aryan" women. So this identifiable obsession in the history of racist currents has attempted to deny the evidence, i.e., the basic unity of humanity, and has, moreover, spread to other differences, such as social differences. It is well known that, ultimately, a woman of the ruling class was not supposed to marry, or even have a sexual relationship, let alone children, with a man from the working classes. The masters were not supposed to reproduce the species with the slaves, and so on. In other words, there were long periods of time when asserting the unity of the species amounted to a social scandal.

If we assert the unity of humanity as such against all forms of racism and segregation, be it racial, national, religious, or social (class-based, let's say), then what becomes of the question of otherness, the question of the Other? What is the Other in general terms if we assume that there are no such differences in the basic foundation of the human species' existence? How can we assert the existence of the Other in the retained element of the Same, if we accept the principle of the basic unity of humanity?

As you know, there are still many places, many parts of the world, where the inferiority of women, of a particular group, of other countries, of a particular religion, or a particular complex of customs is taken for granted. And there are many places, including right here, it must be said, where people are prone to pride themselves on having a superior civilization, think they're the salt of the earth, and claim that our so-called "democratic" system of government is the best one in the history of the planet, not just now but forever.

Just as an aside, the current sorry spectacle of our presidential election should take us down a peg or two in this regard, don't you think?

But perhaps the most important issue today is the dominant social organization – indeed, even more dominant in that it has now taken over the whole human adventure, the whole global space.

It is called "capitalism" – that's its official name – and it creates monstrous forms of inequality, and therefore of otherness, within the basic unity of the human species, to which it may very well also lay claim. There are some familiar statistics on this that I nevertheless often repeat because we need to know them. Actually, it can all be summed up in one sentence: today, a very small global oligarchy is practically depriving billions of human beings of the chance to simply survive, forcing them to roam the world in search of a place to work, provide for their families, and so on.

So the fact that humanity is only at the very beginning of its historical existence may hinge on this. What I mean is that its dominant organization, in terms of social relations, of practical humanity, real humanity, is still extremely weak. That humanity is still Neolithic means that it is not yet the case that humanity, in terms of what it produces, creates, and organizes, lives up in any way to its fundamental unity. Perhaps humanity's historical existence involves testing and producing models of collective existence that live up to the principle of its basic unity. Perhaps we are only in the trial-and-error and still-tentative stages of this project.

Sartre once said that if humanity proved to be incapable of achieving communism – this was back when that word was used innocently, so to speak – then, after humanity died out, it could be said that it had been of no more interest than ants. It's easy to see what he meant. The collective hierarchical economy of ants is known to be a despotic model of organization, so he meant that if we survey human history from above with the idea that humanity should and could produce a social organization worthy of its basic unity, that is, produce a conscious affirmation of itself as a unified species, then the total failure of that endeavor would reduce humanity to being just one animal figure among others, to being an animal figure that is still dominated by the struggle for survival, competition among individuals, and the triumph of the fittest.

Let me put it another way. There clearly needs to be, *there will have to be, in the current centuries, and on a scale that we can't comprehend, a second revolution after the Neolithic Revolution.* A revolution that, by its sheer magnitude, would be on a par with the Neolithic Revolution but that would restore humanity's fundamental unity in the proper order of the immanent organization of

society. The Neolithic Revolution gave humanity unprecedented means of communication and
subsistence as well as conflicts and knowledge,
but it did not eliminate – far from it, and in
certain respects it exacerbated – inequalities,
hierarchies, and figures of violence and power,
which it increased on an unprecedented scale.
This second revolution (I'm defining it very gen-
erally here; we're still at a pre-political level, so
to speak) would allow humanity's unity, that
undeniable unity, to regain control over its own
destiny. Humanity's unity would no longer be
just a fact and would become in a way a norm,
since humanity would have to assert and achieve
its own humanity instead of producing it in the
figure of differences, inequalities, and fragmenta-
tions of all sorts – national, religious, linguistic,
and so on. The second revolution would eliminate the – actually criminal – motive, where
humanity's unity is concerned, of the inequality
of wealth and ways of life.

It could be said that since the French Revolution
of 1792–4 there has been no lack of attempts to
achieve real equality, under a variety of names,
such as "democracy," "socialism," "communism." It could also be considered that the current

temporary triumph of a global capitalist oligarchy represents a failure of those attempts, but we can assume that this failure is only provisional and proves nothing, if regarded, of course, from the perspective of the unity of humanity as such. A problem like this can't be resolved by the next election (nothing, in fact, can); it is on the scale of centuries. And ultimately there is nothing else to say about this except "We've failed, so let's keep up the fight."

The fact remains that humanity, like all species, moreover, is made up of individuals. So, on this microscopic (so to speak) scale, the question of the Other, and even a certain absoluteness of this question, would appear to be unavoidable. There's the overall unity of humanity in its biological and historical adventure dimension, on the one hand, and, on the other, there's humanity's microscopic composition as individuals, about whom we always have to say that, in some sense, there's I, who am the Same as myself, and there are other people, who belong to the category of the Other. Rimbaud, of course, said: "I is an other," and we'll see that, in a sense, that's true. But we must nonetheless note, to begin with, that I can live according to sexual, matrimonial, family, political, linguistic, and ideological customs that are very different from those existing elsewhere. I can die, and others survive. I can rejoice, and others suffer, or vice versa. No doubt I constantly experience my similarities with other people, but also my differences from them, which means that I can't avoid experiencing my own uniqueness.

As you know, even biologically, after all, this uniqueness is confirmed by genetic mapping, and however many the identical traits in this domain – they are extremely plentiful – it is still the case that the proof that I am irreducibly, if only minimally, different from any other person is encoded in my DNA.

So, in connection with this irreducibility of the self, with the relationship between one human animal and another, I would now like to examine four very different texts: one by Victor Hugo, one by Sartre, one by Lacan, and one by Hegel. This is a path that leads from the asserted Same to the dialecticized Other.

I'll start with Hugo because he allows me to segue quite smoothly back to the concept of humanity's unity with which I began. The text is a very famous passage from the Preface to *The*

*Contemplations.* I'm sure you're all familiar with it, but let me just remind you of it:

> None of us has the honor of having a life all his own. My life is yours, your life is mine, you live what I live; destiny is one. Take this mirror and look at yourself in it. People sometimes complain about writers who say "I." "Speak to us about us," they cry. Alas! When I speak to you about myself, I am speaking to you about yourself. How is it you don't see that? Ah, you fool, who think that I am not you!

Here, Hugo, with his remarkable rhetoric, invokes the thesis that the sameness of humanity's destiny is actually reflected as well in the relationship between the Self and the Other. We could say that the poet, unlike the biologist or the scientist, sees, through his own unique linguistic lens, that the unity of humanity is in a way reflected in a profound identity between human lives, a sort of invariability, regardless of the individual particularity of these lives. This could be called the empathic vision of the Other, namely that in every human life I see a profound identity with my own, an identity that, on the microscopic level, reflects the general – or generic, we could say – identity of humanity as a whole. Ultimately, a human life, as seen by Hugo, does not differ fundamentally from the human adventure as a whole, since I can tell, by a sort of immediate feeling, that there is a common impulse between the Other's life and my own, regardless of how their details may differ.

The operative word here is "life." In what sense can it be said that life – what an individual becomes over time – defines the individual's uniqueness? This is Hugo's underlying premise: what is called life, the individual's life, is the ground on which something happens that, like the human adventure as a whole, is generic in nature. Something that actually makes no essential difference. Everything hinges here on the answer to the following question: Can we assume that an individual is reducible to their life? It's an odd question, but it's to this question that Hugo implicitly replies: "Yes, we can; we must." An individual is wholly exhausted by their life – their life, or, in other words, what they do, what they are, what they dream.

I think something could be objected to this vision. It could be objected that an individual's actual life may not have been such that they could achieve everything they were capable of, for external reasons. In other words, otherness can come from outside in the sense of cutting an individual off from what they are really capable of, which wasn't able to be expressed in their actual life. We could say that an individual is obviously a life, but that the individual's life is not necessarily the translation of the real potential, and therefore the inner being, of the individual. An individual can in some respects be cut off from their own life or cut off from themself by life. And in that case, to simply say: "I recognize in the Other their similarity to me because they have the same life as I have" wouldn't do, because it could be argued that an individual is an infinite number of possibilities not all of which are realized and a great many of which, perhaps for external reasons – social relations, for example, or inequality, and so on – are not realizable. But does that mean we can remove this unrealizable portion of immanent possibilities from the definition of the individual? Wouldn't that be a mutilation of their real being? It's a question worth considering.

Ultimately, that is the limitation of what could be called the humanistic theory of the Other, which is clearly Hugo's theory: namely, the idea that, through the mediation of life, I connect with the fundamental unity of the species, thanks to a sort of empathy or vital recognition. I personally think that "life" is too broad a term, too much like purely species, as opposed to individual, determinations. To invoke "life" is to use a mesh that is too large to trap the fine distinctions of individual uniqueness, especially since, for external reasons, they may have been reduced to unrealized potentialities. And I'll conclude on this point by saying that there is nothing more important, when considering the achievement of the equality of human lives, than taking into account what inflicts weakness on them from the outside. Overcoming these weaknesses is a problem that cannot be resolved solely with the category of life as observed from the outside. Rather, it has to do with a reserve or a resource of that life. So much for the first text, by Hugo.

The second is a sentence of Lacan's, as usual a sentence in his somewhat mysterious style. It is: "All desire is desire of the Other." "Other" with a capital O.

This time, the individual is approached – and you can see how this ties in with my previous comment – by way of their desire, which is a more precise word than "life." The word "life" is obviously totalizing, while "desire" is something that connotes the uniqueness of an outward projection. All desire is indeed desire of something, desire for what Lacan calls the object of desire, which he writes as small *a* for "*autre*," [meaning "other," but which, in English, is usually left untranslated as "*objet petit a*"]. With the category of desire, we apprehend the individual not through the objective vicissitudes of their life but through the figure that projects them, whether successfully or otherwise, towards the outside world, and especially towards the Other. This is what Lacan's statement suggests first: All desire is desire *of* the Other. Therefore, individual difference incorporates the diversity of the world, the diversity of others, and the imaginary as well, in the form of make-believe, non-existent, fantasy objects, which can nevertheless be objects of desire.

As you can see, otherness exceeds individuality in this vision while at the same time constituting it. Because desire is desire of the Other, the Other is something necessary for the construction of subjectivity. So they can no longer be construed merely as an objective resource. But the subtlety of the sentence actually hinges on the ambiguity of the French preposition *de*, because *désir* de *l'autre* can mean not only the desire of or for the Other but also another person's desire. *Tout désir est désir de l'autre* can mean: all desire is the desire of or for the Other, that is, all desire is the desire for the Other's desire, ultimately. Or some such thing. So, in that case, desire, in terms of the relationship to the Other, is conceived of as desire of the desire. It's a common experience, after all, to feel that desire, deep down, is the desire for the Other's desire, the desire to obtain the Other's desire. And thus, what we have here is the constitution of a dependence on the Other at the heart of the subject themself, a dependence that's not just objective but subjective. The Same is dependent on the Other not just in terms of resources, or possibilities, or the social relationship, and so on, but at their deepest level, namely, desire. They are in a sense already connected to the Other in the mediation of their own desire. If my desire is desire for the Other's desire, if, for example (and this is frequently the case), my desire is the desire for the Other to desire me, then my desire consists in objectifying the Other's desire, since

I constitute the Other's desire as the object of my own desire. Therefore, the subjective figure of the Other is constituted as an object by my desire, as the object of my desire very precisely, but without any kind of guarantee that the Other as an individual will accept this objectification, because for them, for the Other, their desire is in fact subjective. And so the constitution of the subjectivity of this desire as an object may be experienced as an inadmissible objectification. Finally, what happens in Lacan's sentence is that the Other actually becomes the central enigma of desire insofar as they are always responsible, in one way or another, for my desire. It is always from the perspective of the Other's desire that something that is responsible for my own desire must be said.

This is a process of subjective internalization of otherness. Otherness, outside the individual, is no longer simply an external or constrained relationship, or a submission, or a difference; rather, the Other becomes an enigma of the subject themself precisely because they are an enigma of desire, and desire always demands a response.

We are making progress here on a very important point, which is that the question of the individual, from the point of view of otherness, is clearly a question of identity, except that this identity contains the Other within it. In other words, no identity can do without otherness. The very important lesson we learn from this is that it is always a fantasy, and sometimes a criminal one, to think that there can be identity without otherness. The thesis of the elimination of otherness may lead, and has historically led, to bloodshed, from the moment that, instead of understanding that since all desire is the desire of the Other, the Other is internal to my own desire, I instead assume the Other to be external, to be a border at which my desire is forever rejected, and so I attempt to destroy them.

In terms of the point we started from, this means that, for humanity to be reflected in its unity at the level of subjective interiority itself, it is extremely important to understand that the Other is a figure of the subject themselves and not just something that can appear or be reduced to the object of their desire, or a service rendered, or a purely dialogic exteriority. This is clearly what psychoanalysis has shown on a grand scale; it is its fundamental contribution. It has closely studied how the symbolic construction of a subject makes the Other an inner category of this construction and any attempt to expel otherness and purify the subject a criminal and/or suicidal endeavor.

In the third text, by Sartre, negative consequences will be drawn from this. It will ultimately be assumed that the Other's presence within me, the internal coercion this presence exerts, is actually a sort of curse of all humanity. This passage is from the end of *No Exit*, a play by Sartre, which is also very famous. Let me just give you a little background. Three people, two women and a man, are locked in a room. The man has left one of the women for the other – the plot of a farce, in a way – and this farcical plot is based on scenes that go around in circles, with no way out, the man being unable to decide for himself who the essential Other is; one of the women being jealous because she thinks the other woman is in fact that essential Other internal to the construction of the male subject; and the second woman being resentful that the first one is jealous, and so on. A sort of endless circulation is thus created. And after a while, the three characters realize that this circularity is eternal, that they are in Hell, and will be forever. Let me read you the end. The male character is speaking:

I tell you everything's been thought out before-
hand. They knew [*who the "they" is, the evil powers
of humanity's destiny, is left an open question*] I'd
stand at the fireplace stroking this thing of bronze,
with all those eyes intent on me. Devouring me
. . . What? Only two of you? I thought there were
more; many more. So this is hell. I'd never have
believed it. You remember all we were told about
the torture chambers, the fire and brimstone, the
"burning marl." Old wives' tales! There's no need
for burning pokers. Hell is – other people!

You see, for Sartre, the Other is present in the
basic constitution of consciousness. We are deal-
ing here, too, with the internalization of the
problem of the Other, but in an intrinsic, constitutive way. This is what he calls "the for-others."
Every consciousness is defined on the one hand as
being for-itself, reflective. We read the following
in Sartre's most important book of philosophy:
"Consciousness is a being *such that in its being,*
its being is in question [. . .]" Consciousness is
thus reflective self-effectuation. But, on the other
hand, it is also pure intentionality, hence a direct
relationship to what is external to it. The complete sentence is: "Consciousness is a being *such*

*that in its being*, its being is in question insofar as this being implies a being other than itself." Note, by the way, that there is an overuse of the word "being" in this sentence to mean the being proper to consciousness, about which Sartre will correctly conclude that it is in fact nothingness. Consciousness, exhausted from searching in vain for its being, from going over and over the intractable question of its being, realizes that its true operation, its unfindable being, is nihilation. And this nihilating operation is Sartre's definition of freedom.

In any case, for Sartre, my relationship to others is constitutive. In particular, the being of consciousness is related to a conscious being other than itself, so the relationship to another consciousness is always constitutive of the being of consciousness. There are two main alternatives when it comes to this relationship to others. My desire, in the first case, is to objectify the Other, to treat them as an object, to reduce their subjective dimension to that of an object through which I apprehend myself as free. Why do I apprehend myself as free through this experience? Because everything that is *not* freedom has been projected into the Other. I make the Other bear the fate of slavery, and since I do, I'm the one who possesses freedom, which is mine and mine alone. Sartre calls this figure "sadism," in an obviously ontological sense, in a broad sense. Alternatively, my desire is to turn myself into an object for the Other so that my freedom consists in being dependent on the Other's freedom. My freedom in that case asserts itself as the reduction of and interference with the Other's freedom. The aim is to force the Other to act in such a way that I am only an object for them, whereby I manipulate them – freely, in fact – so as to impose a fiction of enslavement on their freedom. That's masochism.

In actual fact, the relation to the Other in this version, in the Sartre of this period (he later changed his mind to some extent), the twin alternatives of this relationship to the Other, namely, sadism and masochism, is easy to understand. They are two possible positions of freedom. Either I exercise my freedom by reducing consciousness to a state of pure nothingness, by expelling being-in-itself from myself and offloading it onto the Other, or I do the opposite: I interfere with the Other's nothingness through the fiction that I am, freely, a pure object, an in-itself.

The problem is that these two tendencies may not interrelate at all and may constitute the conscious subject as an impasse if the Other, or the others, don't play the same game as I. And the impact of the complexity of the games played on the figure of the Other is what is called "hell" in the play, because these games have no ultimate solution. Freedom can only exist if the Other responds to my demand, but since this is also the case with theirs, they, too, cannot exist as a free subjectivity unless I respond to their demand. If the demands intersect, then there's what Sartre calls a revolving door [*un tourniquet*]. And, at bottom, the relation to the Other often takes the form of a revolving door. You've all experienced arguments, and if you take a close look at them, they're always revolving doors, lovers' quarrels first and foremost. They're always revolving doors where each person tries to pin the blame on the other. Of course, since each of you digs your heels in, you can go around and around forever, until all you can say is: we'll never see eye to eye – of course you won't, since the argument goes around in circles. So what Sartre calls subjective hell is being like a caged animal who can only keep going around and around as in a revolving door, the revolving door of the duality of the relation to the Other, the reversibility of sadism and masochism. It is freedom itself that creates the revolving door of the relation to the Other because that is the fate of its being.

We have thus carried out a sort of survey of the impasses, since, in a way, the humanistic figure of empathy comes up against the fact that interiority hides capacities that are not necessarily evident in life as it is, while, in what we have just been exploring, dependence on the Other is, on the contrary, extreme, but at the same time it generates figures of vital impossibility or of hopeless, revolving-door circularity.

To get out of these impasses we need to go back to the original formulation of the problem by Hegel. Indeed – and this is a very interesting historical issue – for a long period in the history of philosophy, the question of the Other, in terms of the Other as another subject, another mind, another consciousness, another figure of humanity, was not formulated as such or at any rate did not have the central position it later had. This is probably because the theory of the subject remained largely confined within a substantial theory of the soul, the effect of which was that, in classical metaphysics, there was a tendency for the objectification of subjectivity as such, its interiority, to prevail over its dependence or its externalization. That is what the word "soul" has more or less always meant. An individual is a soul, essentially. But the soul, metaphysically, is a substance related to the body in a complex way, or else it is a form of the body, and that's even more complicated. None of this creates a real space for exploring the dialectic of the Other.

Admittedly, there is an amazing dialectic of the Other in Plato's *Sophist*, but it is a theory of ontological categories, not a theory of others. The theory of the Other in Plato, as opposed to Parmenides, leads to the need for a figure of not-being so that the Other can differ from the Same. But this theory is not applied directly to the problem of human relations per se, to a thinking of others.

It is important to recognize that it was in the eighteenth century that this became a problem formulated as such in the history of Western metaphysics. And it was formulated in a way I would not exactly call definitive, but fundamental, by Hegel in the *Phenomenology of Spirit*. It was the famous master–slave dialectic.

A complete analysis of the master–slave dialectic would be a lecture in its own right, and anyway, I'm going to assume you're somewhat familiar with it. I'd like to quote only the pivotal sentence from it and comment briefly on it. That sentence is: "Self-consciousness exists in itself and for itself, in that, and by the fact that it exists for another self-consciousness [. . .]" Actually, Hegel offered an earlier, positive version of the revolving-door analogy that Sartre came up with – Sartre who, by the way, was directly inspired by Hegel. This is what I'd like to highlight. Hegel's version can't be equated with Sartre's because Hegel's is a complex process, not a simple structural figure. For Hegel, the relationship of one consciousness to another is not a structure, as is the revolving door of sadism and masochism; it's a process, or, you could almost say, a story.

For Hegel, consciousness is, on the one hand, a being; it is in itself, and, on the other hand, it is a reflection; it is for itself. This is obviously the classic theme of the scissiparity of consciousness insofar as it can be apprehended as something that exists in itself, but at the same time, being reflective, sees itself as in itself for itself. However, in order for its reflective being to be integrated with its objective being, that is, in order for it to see itself as in itself and for itself, another consciousness has to have reflected this reflection, as constitutive of the being of the other consciousness.

So what does this mean? In very simple terms, it means that if an individual is not just an object but a consciousness, that is, a reflection; if they are for themself; if they relate to themself as a thinking interiority, then, in order for them to fully realize that they are such, another consciousness, which reflects this reflection as constitutive of their being, is needed. In other words, it is in the encounter between two consciousnesses that each consciousness is constituted as a consciousness.

It is clear that there is an absolute essentiality to the encounter with the Other. If there were no encounter with the Other, the reflective dimension of consciousness would somehow remain an inert part of the in-itself. What activates it, what makes it present to itself as what it is, is the fact that another consciousness apprehends it as participating in the being of the Other.

At the same time, the judgments that constitute reflectivity as objective from the Other's point of view may be and usually are judgments of all kinds, including negative ones. For example, you run into someone you know, and you say (this is one example among others): "Oh, that guy's got a very high opinion of himself!" What are you doing? You're saying, first of all, that he is in-himself, since he is definable as having that idea, but he is also for-himself, since he has a high opinion of himself. So you freeze him, you constitute him as an individual as the sum of an objective and a reflective existence. That's what Hegel describes very simply, in his own lexicon. But, clearly, each person will relate to the Other in this way, so each will expect the Other to recognize them as a reflective objectivity: in particular, I will expect the Other to recognize me for what *I* think I am. And since each expects this recognition from the Other, there is a conflict. This is what Hegel calls the struggle for recognition. It is the dialectic of this struggle for recognition that will constitute the complete schema of constitution of the individual as a self-consciousness, the individual who will exact full recognition from the Other. And what Hegel explains is that there is a preliminary winner of this struggle, and that this winner will make the Other work for them in a variety of ways: that's why it's called the master–servant (or lord–bondsman) dialectic. It probably ought to be translated along the lines of "domination" and "submission." Terms like "master," "bondsman," and "slave" shouldn't be taken literally. The Other can be made to work for you in many different ways; it doesn't necessarily have to be by making them dig the ground and grow wheat for you. The Other can be made to work for you because you've exacted recognition of what you are from them, and, in this respect, you have it over them because *you* don't have to recognize *them*. This is an experience anyone can have, and so there are actually all kinds of ways to be put to work in the service of someone by the figure of recognition. It can be subjective work, dependence, and so on.

If we were to leave it at that, we would have roughly the Sartrean schema, because the Sartrean schema says: the person who won the struggle for recognition is the sadist, and the person who is content not to have been recognized is the masochist. But that is not at all what Hegel says; he says that the person who works is actually the real winner. Indeed, the person who works to maintain their position must invent and create, while all the Other does is sit around in their easy chair being admired and recognized. Hegel even goes much further since he explains – but here I'm only giving the briefest sketch of these absolutely amazing passages – that, actually, the one who is the slave, the bondsman, who works for the master or lord, is the one who will invent a new figure of thought. The one who, simply to survive in this very difficult situation of not being recognized, will invent a new culture. That's Hegel's word. So intellectual creativity, in Hegel's eyes, is a capacity of the person from whom a master has exacted what is ultimately false recognition, since what will prevail in the end, what will be recognized by everyone, will be the result of the work of the one who was dominated.

Once we've understood that the person who works, invents, and creates becomes, within the context of otherness, the master of their master through their own capacity for creative invention, we can ultimately return to the original description. What we learn is that otherness is immanent in all identity, which means that I am only myself insofar as I am the Other of that Other for whom I am myself. There's no getting around this, and it is the real foundation of freedom. That's what Hegel means: the free person isn't the master. When all is said and done, the free person is the slave, because to be free is to create something out of one's situation and not to settle into its false eternity.

I am free only if I recognize the Other's freedom, so that is the foundation of freedom. But otherness is also the foundation of fraternity because we are together with one another inasmuch as each of us is the Other's Other. Fraternity is a method of recognizing otherness within identity. That's what fraternity is: recognizing that within identity, within what we have in common, there is still otherness. And otherness is clearly also the foundation of equality. There is no one I could consider more Other than I myself am and therefore less human than I am. So, liberty, equality, and fraternity are in every case different ways of saying that otherness is immanent within all identity and consequently that the project of humanity as a whole – the aim of the new revolution that will get us out of the Neolithic era, that will allow humanity to match its collective organization to its essential, original unity – that this project, then, is based on the key issue of the immanence of otherness rather than its exteriority. Thus, the

Other is the touchstone of affirmative existence, which indeed affirms, and achieves, the unity of humanity. That is why the Other – the foreigner, the nomadic proletarian, the refugee – is the main category of any true politics, that is, of any politics directed toward and by the second revolution. Any politics of this sort is a mobilization of the category of the Other in specific forms. The Other, through which our commonality is realized as communism. The Other, so that, due to the post-Neolithic Revolution, something different may finally emerge in history. Humanity has organized itself on the principle that it must be recognized everywhere as the same, in every other person as in myself, in every-one, and must share everywhere what it has in it that is common to us all. After the Neolithic Revolution, which created humanity as it still is today – resourceful and ingenious, master over nature and ubiquitous, but full of inequality and ferocious – will come, must come, the second revolution, the communist revolution.

# Thirteen Theses and Some Comments on Politics Today

***Thesis 1.*** *The current world situation is characterized by the territorial and ideological hegemony of liberal capitalism.*

**Comment:** This thesis is so obvious and banal that there is no need for me to comment on it.

***Thesis 2.*** *This hegemony is by no means in critical condition, let alone in an irreversible coma; rather, it is in a particularly intense phase of its development.*

**Comment:** With regard to capitalist globalization, which is totally hegemonic today, there are two theses as antithetical as they are false. The first is the conservative thesis: capitalism, especially when combined with parliamentary "democracy," is the ultimate form of human economic and social organization. It is indeed the end of history, in Fukuyama's sense. The second is the thesis that capitalism has entered its final crisis, or even the thesis that it is already dead.

The first thesis is nothing but the repetition of the ideological process begun in the late 1970s by the renegade intellectuals of the so-called "red years" (1965–75), which consisted in purely and simply eliminating the communist hypothesis from the field of possibilities. It has made it possible to simplify the dominant propaganda: there is no longer any need to sing the (dubious) praises of capitalism but only to maintain that the facts (the USSR, Lenin, Stalin, Mao, China, the Khmer Rouge, the Western Communist parties, etc.) have shown that nothing other than a criminal "totalitarianism" was possible.

In the face of this verdict of impossibility, the only action required of us is to reinstate, by assessing and going beyond the piecemeal experiments of the past century, the communist hypothesis in all its possibility, force, and liberating potential. This is what is happening now and will inevitably happen in the future, and it's what I'm trying to do in this very essay.

The two forms of the second thesis – exhausted capitalism or dead capitalism – are often based on the financial crisis of 2008 and on the countless episodes of corruption revealed every day. They conclude either that the time is ripe for revolution, that all it would take is one strong push for the whole "system" to come crashing down, or even that all we'd have to do is step aside, retreat – to the country, for example – and we'd then realize that our new "forms-of-life" can be developed there, with the capitalist machine running on empty in its ultimate nullity.

None of this has the slightest relationship to reality.

First of all, the 2008 crisis was a classic crisis of overproduction (too many houses were built in the United States and sold on credit to insolvent people), whose spread, given the necessary time, brought fresh impetus to capitalism, which was cleaned up and invigorated by a strong period of capital concentration, with the weak bled dry, the strong beefed up, and, in the process – a major benefit – the "social legislation" from the end of World War II largely liquidated. The "recovery" is currently in sight, now that this painful clean-up is complete.

Secondly, the extension of capitalist domination to vast areas of the world, the intensive and extensive diversification of the global market, is far from complete. Nearly all of Africa, much of Latin America, Eastern Europe, and India: these are all places "in transition," either looting zones or "emerging" economies, in which large-scale market implantation can and must follow the example of Japan or China.

Thirdly, the very essence of capitalism is corruption. How could a social system whose only rules are "profit first" and worldwide dog-eat-dog competition avoid widespread corruption? Corruption "cases" are nothing but side operations, either local purges for propaganda purposes or the result of a settling of scores between rival cliques.

In reality, modern capitalism, the capitalism of the global market, which, at only a few hundred years old, is historically a very recent social formation, is only just beginning to conquer the planet, after a colonial period (from the sixteenth to the twentieth century) during which the conquered lands were subservient to the limited, protectionist market of a single country. Today, the looting has become globalized, as has the proletariat, which now comes from every country in the world.

*Thesis 3. Three active contradictions are undermining this hegemony.*

*1. The highly developed oligarchic dimension of capital ownership leaves less and less latitude for new owners to join the oligarchy, hence there is a possibility of authoritarian sclerosis.*

*2. The integration of financial and commercial networks into a single world market is opposed, where the policing of the masses is concerned, by the maintenance of national entities that invariably compete with one another, hence there is a possibility of a world war so that one clearly hegemonic country might emerge, including on the world market.*

*3. There is doubt today that, given its current line of development, Capital can put the workforce of the entire world population to work, hence there is the risk that a mass of completely destitute and consequently politically dangerous people might develop worldwide.*

**Comment:** Regarding the first point, there are currently 264 people – and the concentration of wealth continues unabated – who own as much as three billion other people do. Right here in France, 10% of the population owns well over 50% of the total wealth. Such concentrations of wealth are unprecedented in human history. And they are not over, not by a long shot. There is something monstrous about them, which obviously means they won't last forever, but which is inherent in capitalist development and is even the main driving force behind it.

Regarding the second point, US hegemony is increasingly under siege. China and India alone possess 40% of the global workforce, which is indicative of devastating deindustrialization in the West. Indeed, American workers now only account for 7% of the total workforce, and Europe even less. As a result of these disparities, the world order, still dominated for military and financial reasons by the United States, is seeing the emergence of rivals who want their share of power over the world market. Clashes have already broken out, in the Middle East, Africa, and the South China Sea. There will be more of them. The outcome of such a situation can only be war, as the slaughters of the past century have amply demonstrated.

Regarding the third point, already today there are probably between two and three billion people who are neither capitalist owners, nor landless peasants, nor wage earners belonging to a petty bourgeoisie, nor workers. They roam the world in search of a place to live, and they constitute a nomadic proletariat which, if politicized, would become a very significant threat to the established order.

*Thesis 4. Over the past ten years, there have been numerous, sometimes forceful, revolts against this or that aspect of the hegemony of liberal capitalism. But they have also been suppressed without significant difficulty.*

**Comment:** These movements have been of four types.

1. Short-lived, localized riots. There have been large, spontaneous riots on the outskirts of big cities such as London and Paris, usually in response to police killings of young men. Either these riots had no broad support in a fearful public opinion and were ruthlessly put down, or they were followed by huge "humanitarian" mobilizations, focused on police violence and largely depoliticized.

2. Sustained uprisings but with no organizational innovation. Other movements, especially in the Arab world, were much broader socially and lasted for many weeks. They took the iconic form of occupations of public squares. Their numbers were usually reduced by the temptation of elections. The most typical case was Egypt's: a massive movement, the apparent success of the negative unifying slogan "Mubarak, get out!" (Mubarak stepped down and was even arrested), the prolonged inability of the police to regain control of the square, the explicit unity of Coptic Christians and Muslims, the apparent neutrality of the army, and so on. But, of course, in the elections it was the party that was active among the masses – and not very much so in the movement – namely, the Muslim Brotherhood, that won. The most militant section of the movement opposed this new government and thus paved the way for the intervention of the army, which put a general, Al-Sisi, back in power. He ruthlessly suppressed all the opposition movements, the Muslim Brotherhood first and then the young revolutionaries, and actually restored the old regime, in a worse form than before. The circular nature of this episode is particularly striking.

3. Movements leading to the creation of a new political force. In some cases, the movement was able to create the conditions for the emergence of a new political force, different from the old parliamentary hacks. This was the case with Syriza in Greece, where the riots had been particularly numerous and severe, and with Podemos in Spain. These forces dissolved by themselves in parliamentary consensus. In Greece, the new government, headed by Tsipras, gave in to the European Commission's demands without much of a fight and led the country back down the path of endless austerity measures. In Spain, Podemos, too, got trapped in the game of alliances, whether with the majority or the opposition. Not a trace of genuine politics emerged from these organizational innovations.

4. Relatively long-term movements but with no significant positive impact. In some cases, aside from a few classic tactical episodes (such as the "bypassing" of conventional demonstrations by groups equipped to confront the police for a few minutes), the lack of political innovation has led to the rehabilitation of the figure of conservative reaction at global level. This is the case in the United States, for example, where the predomi-

nant counter-effect of the "Occupy Wall Street" movement was Trump's coming to power, or even in France, where the end result of the "Nuit debout" movement is Macron.

*Thesis 5. The reason for this weakness in the movements of the past decade is the absence of politics, or even the hostility to politics, in a variety of forms and identifiable by a number of symptoms.*

**Comment:** In particular, the following should be noted as signs of a very weak political subjectivity:

1. Unifying slogans that are exclusively negative: "against" this or that, "Mubarak, get out," "Down with the oligarchy of the 1%," "Say no to the Labor law," "No one likes the police," and so on.

2. The lack of a broad temporality: both in terms of knowledge of the past – virtually absent from the movements, aside from a few caricatures, and no creative assessment of which is proposed – and projection into the future, limited to abstract considerations about liberation or emancipation.

3. Terminology heavily borrowed from the enemy. This is mainly the case with a particularly ambiguous category like "democracy," or the use

of the category of "life," "our lives," which is just an ineffective investment in the collective action of existential categories.

4. Blind worship of "novelty" and contempt for established truths. This comes straight out of the commercial cult of the "novelty" of products and out of a persistent belief that something is being "started" that has already happened many times before. It simultaneously prevents people from learning from the past, from understanding how structural repetitions work, and from not falling for fake "modernities."

5. An absurd time scale. This scale, modeled on the Marxist circular flow of "money-commodities-money," assumes that problems like private property or the pathological concentration of wealth, which have resisted resolution for millennia, will be dealt with or even resolved in a matter of a few weeks of "the movement." The failure to see that much of capitalist modernity is merely a modern version of the triad established several thousand years ago, right from the time of the Neolithic "Revolution," namely: Family, Private Property, State. And therefore that the communist system, in terms of the central problems that constitute it, is on a scale of centuries.

6. A weak relationship to the state. What is involved here is a constant underestimation of the state's resources as compared with those of a given "movement," in terms of both armed force and the potential for corruption. In particular, the effectiveness of "democratic" corruption, the symbol of which is electoral parliamentarianism, is underestimated, as is the extent of the ideological domination of this corruption where the overwhelming majority of the population is concerned.

7. A patchwork of different approaches with no assessment of their effectiveness in either the distant or recent past. No conclusion that can be widely popularized is drawn from methods that have been used since at least the "red years" (1965–75) at any rate, or even for the past two hundred years, such as the occupation of factories, union strikes, legal demonstrations, the formation of groups whose purpose is to enable local confrontation with the police, the seizure of buildings, the sequestration of bosses in factories, and so on. Nor is any conclusion drawn from their stationary counterparts: for example, long, repetitive hyper-democratic gatherings in public squares crowded with people, where everyone,

regardless of their ideas and linguistic aptitude, is obliged to speak for three minutes, the ultimate aim being only the repetition of the same activity.

**Thesis 6.** *We need to remember the most important experiments of the recent past and reflect on why they failed.*

**Comment:** From the "red years" to the present.

The comment regarding Thesis 5 probably seems quite polemical, or even pessimistic and depressing, especially to young people who may well be excited, for a while, about all forms of action, whose critical re-examination I'm calling for. You'll understand the reason for such a critique if you bear in mind that I myself experienced and enthusiastically participated in absolutely similar things in May '68 and thereafter, and that I had a chance to observe them long enough to assess their shortcomings. So I have the feeling that the recent movements are wasting their energy repeating, as if they were new, well-known episodes of what can be called "the right wing" of the May '68 movement, regardless of whether this right wing grew out of the conventional left wing or the anarchist ultra-left wing that in its own way was already talking about "forms-of-life" and whose militants we called "anarcho-desirers."

There were actually four different movements in '68:

1. A student youth revolt.

2. A revolt of young workers from the large factories.

3. A general union strike attempting to control the two previous revolts.

4. The emergence, often under the name of "Maoism" and with many competing organizations, of a new political initiative, whose objective was to establish a unifying diagonal connection between the first two revolts by giving them an ideological and combative force that seemed able to ensure a real political future for them. It did in fact last for at least ten years or so. The fact that it didn't achieve historical stabilization, which I readily acknowledge, shouldn't lead to a repetition of what happened, without people even knowing that they are repeating it.

Let's just remember that in the June 1968 elections the majority voted into power was so reactionary that it was said to be the reincarnation of the post-World War I "blue horizon"[1] majority. The final result of the May–June 2017 elections, with the landslide victory of Macron, an identified lackey of globalized finance capital, ought to make us stop and think about the repetitive aspect of all this.

*Thesis 7. A politics internal to a movement should provide it with five features, concerning the slogans, the strategy, the vocabulary, the existence of a principle, and a clear tactical vision.*

**Comment:**

1. The main slogans should be affirmative, even at the cost of an internal split once the negative unity has been gone beyond.

2. The slogans should be strategically appropriate, meaning that they should be based on an understanding of the earlier stages of the problem that the movement has placed on the agenda.

3. The terminology used should be controlled and consistent. For example, "communism" is

---

[1] "Blue horizon" was the color of the uniforms that had been worn by the former military men who won election to the Chamber of Deputies in overwhelming numbers after the war.

not consistent with "democracy" today; "equality" is not consistent with "freedom;" any positive use of identity terms such as "French" or "international community" or "Islamist" or "Europe" should be banned, as should psychological terms such as "desire," "life," "person," as well as any term related to established state constructions such as "citizen," "voter," and so on.

4. A principle, something I call an "idea," should be constantly tested against the situation, since it presents locally a non-capitalist systemic possibility.

Here, we need to quote Marx defining the exemplary militant in terms of their manner of presence in the movements: "The communists everywhere support every revolutionary movement against the existing social and political order of things. In all these movements they bring to the front, as the leading question in each, the property question, no matter what its degree of development at the time."

5. Tactically, the movement should always be aligned as far as possible with a body capable of meeting to effectively discuss its own perspective and the basis on which it interprets and judges the situation. Political militants, as Marx says,

are part of the general movement; they are not separate and apart from it. But the one way they differ is in their ability to place the movement in the bigger picture and, on that basis, to plan what the next step should be, but also to make no concessions on these two points, nor, under the pretext of unity, to the conservative views that can easily dominate, subjectively, even a large movement. The experience of revolutions has shown that critical political moments occur in a form that most closely resembles the assembly, i.e., the mass meeting, where the decision to be made is elucidated by speakers, who may also go head to head with each other.

**Thesis 8.** *Politics is responsible for ensuring that the spirit of the movements has a duration that is commensurate with the temporality of states and is not just a negative episode in their domination. Its general definition is that it organizes a discussion, among the different components of the people and on the widest possible scale, about the slogans that ought to be both those of permanent propaganda and those of future movements. Politics provides the general framework for such discussions: it is the assertion that there are currently two alternative* *ways for humanity to organize itself, the capitalist way and the communist one. The former is merely the contemporary form of what has been in existence since the Neolithic Revolution of several thousand years ago. The latter proposes a second global, systemic revolution in the becoming of humanity. It proposes an exit from the Neolithic Age.*

**Comment:** Thus, politics involves determining, through extensive discussions, the local slogan that crystallizes these two alternative ways in the situation. As it is local, this slogan can only come from the experience of the masses involved. It is from this that politics learns what can launch the effective struggle locally, by whatever means, for the communist way. So the immediate task of politics is not antagonistic confrontation but rather the continuous, situated investigation of the ideas, slogans, and initiatives capable of locally sustaining the existence of two ways, one of which involves the preservation of what there is and the other, its utter transformation in accordance with egalitarian principles that the new slogan will crystallize. The name of this activity is "mass work." The essence of politics, outside the movement, is mass work.

***Thesis 9.*** *Politics is done with people from every-where. It cannot accept the different forms of social segregation imposed by capitalism.*

**Comment:** This implies, especially with regard to the educated youth, who have always played a key role in the birth of new forms of politics, the need for a continuous effort to connect with the other social groups, particularly the poorest ones, on which the impact of capitalism is the most dev-astating. Under present conditions, both in our country and around the world, priority should be given to the vast nomadic proletariat who arrive, as the peasants from the Auvergne or Brittany once did, in entire waves, at tremendous risk, to try to survive as workers here since they can no longer do so as landless peasants back where they came from. The method, in this case as in every other, involves patient, local investigation – in marketplaces, housing projects, workers' hostels, factories, and so on. It also involves organizing meetings (even very small ones at first), determin-ing slogans and disseminating them, expanding the labor base, confronting the various local con-servative forces, and so on. It is exciting work, once you understand that stubborn determination is the key to it. One important step is to set up schools to disseminate knowledge about the world history of the struggle between the two ways, about its successes and its current obstacles.

What was done by the organizations that emerged for this purpose after May '68 can and must be done again. We need to restore the political diagonal connection I mentioned earlier, which remains today a diagonal connection between the youth movement, a few intellectuals, and the nomadic proletariat. This is already being done, here and there. It is the only truly political task of the present time.

What has changed is the deindustrialization of the suburbs of major cities. That is moreover the source of the far right's working-class support. We need to fight it on site by explaining how and why two generations of workers have been sacrificed in a few years' time and by simultaneously investigating, as far as possible, the opposite process: the extremely aggressive industrialization going on in Asia. The work with the workers in the past and today is clearly international, even here. In this connection, it would be very useful to produce and publish a journal of and for the workers of the world.

**Thesis 10.** *There is no longer any real political organization today. The task is thus to explore ways to rebuild one.*

**Comment:** An organization is responsible for conducting investigations; for coordinating the mass work and the local slogans resulting from it in such a way as to place them in the bigger picture; for expanding the movements and ensuring the long-term maintenance of their effects. An organization is judged not by its form and procedures, the way a state is judged, but by its verifiable ability to do what it is responsible for. One of Mao's dictums is worth quoting here: an organization is something that "gives back to the masses in a clear form what it has received from the masses in a confused form."

**Thesis 11.** *The traditional party form is doomed today because it has defined itself not by its ability to do what Thesis 10 says – mass work – but by its pretension to "represent" the working class, or the proletariat.*

**Comment:** We must break with the logic of representation in all its forms. A political organization must have an instrumental, not a representative, definition. Moreover, "representation" means "the identity of what is represented." But identities must be excluded from the political field.

*Thesis 12. As we have just seen, it is not the relationship to the state that defines politics. Thus, politics takes place "at a distance from" the state. Strategically, however, the state must be smashed because it is the universal guardian of the capitalist way, particularly because it protects the right to the private ownership of the means of production and exchange. As the Chinese revolutionaries during the Cultural Revolution used to say, "We must break with bourgeois law." Consequently, political action vis-à-vis the state is a mixture of distance and negativity. The aim is actually for the state to be gradually surrounded by a hostile public opinion and political positions that have become alien to it.*

**Comment:** The historical assessment of this issue is very complex. For example, the Russian Revolution of 1917 most certainly combined widespread hostility to the Czarist regime, even in the countryside, because of the war; intense, longstanding ideological preparation, especially among the intellectual class; worker revolts that led to genuine mass organizations, called "soviets;" soldier uprisings; and, with the Bolsheviks, a strong, diversified organization, able to hold mass meetings with orators of the highest caliber due to the strength of their conviction and their didactic prowess. It all came to a head in successful insurrections and a terrible civil war that was ultimately won by the revolutionary side despite massive foreign intervention. The Chinese Revolution took a completely different course: a long march through the countryside; the formation of popular assemblies; a real Red Army; the long-term occupation of a remote area in the north of the country, where land and food production reforms were tried out at the same time as the army was being built up; and the whole process lasting about thirty years. Moreover, instead of the Stalinist Terror of the 1930s, there was a mass student and working-class revolt in China against the elite of the Communist Party. I consider this unprecedented movement, called the Proletarian Cultural Revolution, to be the last example of a politics of direct confrontation with figures of state authority. None of this can be transposed to our situation. But one lesson does come through this whole experience: in no case can the state, whatever its form, represent or define the politics of emancipation.

The complete dialectics of every true politics has four components:

1. The strategic Idea of the struggle between the two ways, the communist one and the capitalist one. This is what Mao called the "ideological preparation of public opinion," without which, he said, revolutionary politics is impossible.

2. The local commitment to this idea or principle by the organization, in the form of mass work. The decentralized circulation of all that comes out of this work in terms of slogans and successful practical experiences.

3. Popular movements, in the form of historical events, within which the political organization works for both their negative unity and the refining of their affirmative determination.

4. The state, whose power must be smashed, by confrontation or encirclement, if it is that of the agents of capitalism. And if it derives from the communist way, it must wither away, if necessary by the revolutionary means initiated amid deadly chaos by the Chinese Cultural Revolution.

To devise the contemporary arrangement of

these four components in real-life conditions is the simultaneously practical and theoretical problem of our times.

*Thesis 13. The situation of contemporary capitalism involves a sort of disconnect between the globalization of the market and the still largely national character of the police and military control of populations. In other words, there is a gap between the economic scheme of things, which is global, and its necessary state protection, which is still national. The latter aspect is reviving imperialist rivalries, albeit in different forms. Despite this change in form, the risk of war is growing. War is already happening, moreover, in many parts of the world. Future politics will also be responsible for preventing, if it can, the outbreak of a total war, which could jeopardize the existence of humanity this time. It can also be said that the historic choice is: either humanity breaks with the contemporary Neolithic Age that is capitalism and begins its communist phase on a global scale, or it remains in its Neolithic phase, and it will be in great danger of perishing in a nuclear war.*

**Comment:** On the one hand, the great powers today are trying to cooperate to ensure the stability of world trade, particularly by fighting protectionism, but, on the other hand, they are secretly fighting for their own hegemony. One result of this is the end of blatantly colonial practices such as those carried out by France or England in the nineteenth century, namely, the military and administrative occupation of entire countries. I propose calling the new practice that has replaced the old ones "zoning": in entire zones of the world (Iraq, Syria, Libya, Afghanistan, Nigeria, Mali, Central African Republic, Congo, etc.) governments are destroyed, wiped out, and the area becomes a looting zone, open to both armed bands and all the capitalist predators on the planet. Or else the government is composed of profiteers linked in a thousand ways to major global corporations. The rivalries become entangled over vast areas, with constantly shifting power relations. Given these conditions, all it would take is some rogue military incident for us to be suddenly on the brink of war. The blocs have already been carved out: the United States and their "Western-Japanese" clique on one side, and China and Russia on the other, with nuclear weapons everywhere. So all we can do is remember what Lenin said: "Either revolution will prevent war or war will lead to revolution."

Thus, the highest aspiration of future political work could be defined as follows: that for the first time in history it may be the former possibility – revolution will prevent war – that becomes a reality and not the latter – war will lead to revolution. Indeed, it was the latter possibility that materialized in Russia in the context of the First World War and in China in the context of the Second. But at what a price! And with what long-term consequences!

Let us hope; let us act. Anyone, anywhere, can begin to get involved in true politics, in the sense meant by this essay. And then speak to those around them about what they've done. That's how it all begins.